T0077967

You're Already Infinitely Famous, But it's Still a Cosmic Secret

plus: pleasurably effortless
learning, working, and money,
for everyone, forever

Lewis S. Mancini, MD

 www.trafford.com

North America & international
toll-free: 844-688-6899 (USA & Canada)
fax: 812 355 4082

This book is dedicated to my brother,
Douglas, Christina, Herb and Jane

CONTENTS

About the Author

Now (2017) 66 years old, I've suffered from obsessive-compulsive disorder and bipolar manic depression since 1962, as well as attention deficit disorder and various learning disabilities since birth. While I did manage to graduate from medical school, two years of employment as an intern and resident in a psychiatrist-in-training program, a two-year program in Electroencephalography (EEG) technology and did publish four books and seven articles. However, except for the two years of internship/residency, I've always been too disabled to be gainfully employed. Hence, I've always been on disability or public assistance, of one form or another.

CHAPTER 1

April 2, 2017

The physical laws of conservation of matter and energy indicate no matter or energy can ever be created or destroyed. This validates immortality. Hence, science confirms religion. Actually, You and I and Everyone else are all <u>already</u> and have always been and will always be infinitely and cosmically famous for reasons, which I'll try to begin to explain presently. First, let's hypothesize that you are <u>not</u> your body or your brain. Drs. Jeffrey M. Schwartz, MD and Rebecca Gladding, MD say "You are not your Brain," but don't say what you <u>are</u>. (ref. 1)

Instead, you are a tiny string-shaped particle who is attached to or bonded within your body and brain pair (BBP) and this you-particle moves around within you BBP, integrating all of your experiences, at speeds that might be faster than the speed of light.

This tiny particle is immortal, because in order to age and die, an entity must have component parts into which it can fall apart. And your particle is a unitary something that has no component parts to fall apart into. Hence, it cannot age or die.

Aging is a process whereby your you-particle (YP) gradually falls away from your brain-body pair (BBP) and "dying" (the illusion thereof) is a tearing away of your YP from your BBP.

This tiny you-particle (YP) can be called a mind particle (MP), soul particle (SP), string particle (SP), unconscious or conscious person particle (PP). Since you PP cannot age or die and has always existed intermittently, consequently it has interacted with an infinite number of other PP's. And an infinite number of PPs have interacted with, hence <u>know</u>, your PP.

Since you know an infinite number of immortal PPs and they know YP, you are infinitely famous and, consequently, have always been a significant celebrity, even though that fact is hidden from you throughout your life here on Earth-Hell.

CHAPTER 2

April 7, 2017

Let's hypothesize that every particle of matter in the universe, being a string particle, is equal in quality and worth to every other one. Moreover, all particles have an equal potential to become a person-particle (PP). If your mind is a single particle with its consciousizer switch turned is on, then every mind particle (MP) is equal to both the MP of a genius, a saint and each individual inanimate particle with its consciousizer almost fully turned off that might be part of the furniture or floor that is supporting your weight.

If aging and dying are the processes whereby an object made up of many particles falls apart into its zillions of component particles, then your MP (= PP + experiences), having no component particles, can never age or die (because it has no component particles to fall apart into). Hence, your PP is eternally ageless and immortal.

We have already noted that throughout the course of infinite times, an infinite number of MPs know (enjoy the acquaintance and friendship) of your MP/PP. If virtually everyone knows you and you know virtually everyone, then you and everyone else is infinitely famous and always have/has been and will always be famous. This is one kind of being famous.

A second kind of being famous comes about when any one of an infinite number of universes pops into being via Big Bang implosion-explosion. A universe can only pop into being when the circumstances around it are conducive to all PP/SP/MP participants being ecstatically and heavenly pleasurized. Pleasure, not money, is the currency of every finite Universe. But if all of the participanting PP/SPs within a universe were intensely pleasurized at all times, how could the pleasurable MPs measure time or space <u>without</u> <u>a</u> <u>painful</u> <u>landmark</u> like Earth-Hell to count off time and space against a central point of origin, **x=y=z =0.**

CHAPTER 3

April 9, 2017

Scientist say that there are at least four basic forces in the Universe: **1.** The strong nuclear force, **2.** The weak nuclear force, **3.** Electromagnetism, and **4.** Gravity. But actually, there is <u>only one force </u>(pleasure or the pleasure-pain continuum) and <u>only one</u> kind of <u>matter</u>, which consists in tiny string-shaped as opposed to spherical particles. String shaped particles are more versatile than spherical particles because a string particle can cover infinitely more surface area than a spherical particle can.

God points his finger to a point in space and says, "another finite Universe will begin right here," and every string particle that hears the command, lusting for attention and wanting to be center-stage famous, rushes to that point. God allows only a small percentage of the rushing particles to be center-stage to the new universe. Most of the particles remain and dwell in the intensely envious outer-circler periphery of the new universe, while a small percentage are allowed to live in the true center-stage, inner circular, spherical-area. The inner circle is hell and the outer circle of the finite universe is purgatory. Outside of purgatory, true heaven exists. The downside of the inner circle is that there is pain and suffering liberally intermixed with pleasure and happiness. There is no pain and suffering in the much bigger universal periphery. So those MPs in the center-stage hell (planet) get the pleasure of secret and hidden fame and the punishment of jealousy coming from outer circular peripheral, purgatite mind-soul-string-particles (MSSP)s who get no fame but no other deprivation and get to enjoy every other pleasure.

The single planet-sized center-stage commands the attention of the much bigger, middle-circular periphery. Some suffering is probably necessary because how could the peripheral pleasurites count off time and space so as to cooperate among themselves if there were no attention-grabbing center-stage sufferers? So, every universe (almost) must have suffering at its center (which is a hell) in order to hold the attention of the pleasurable periphery, which is a heaven, as well as Purgatite attention.

Actually, there might be some circumstances where universes can be entirely pleasurable and not at all painful or suffering-full, but we'll get into that possibility later. For now, let's consider the much more common situation of every pleasurable Heaven requiring a painful center-stage hell and a less painful outer-stage Purgatory in order for there to be any cooperation as far as time and space. There can be no cooperation, hence, no Heaven, if we can't agree upon a center-stage temporal and spatial point or planet (e.g., Earth-Hell) of reference.

CHAPTER 4

Aug. 8, 2017

The infinite universe or mega universe includes all of space, time and all finite Universes. Large finite Universes like Ours include a hell which is a single planet, in Our case planet Earth, where there is much suffering. You could say that our Earthly hell was much worse 100,000 years and 100 years ago and you would be correct. The farther back in time you go, the worse things were, and the stranger a belief in Heaven to justify hell there was with life on Earth currently being not too bad, it's easier to be an atheist and the easier it is to believe our current world is almost Heaven. I certainly don't believe contemporary Earth is almost Heaven, instead it seems like mild hell compared to 1,000 years ago.

All of the other planets (except the center stage planet, e.g., Earth-hell) in a large finite universe are devoid of pain and suffering and include only pleasure and happiness. The reason for all the pain and suffering on planet hell (for example, Earth) is that none of the pleasure/happiness could exist unless the pleasureful Heavenly planets could point to a single attention-grabbing place where time is absolute and space equals the "ground zero" of center-stage hell.

The heavenites are so drenched in pleasure and happiness that they would have no reason to pay any attention, let alone count off time and space, in relation to center-stage hell (Earth) unless there were something special about it (i.e., pain and suffering).

So the planet hell marks point time = zero and counting while space = **x=0, y=0**, and **z=0**. So, even though the Heavenites hate the hellites because of their being center-stage, if Earth were just another perfectly pleasureful place, then the Heavenites would have no reason to pay attention to it for the purposes of cooperation and collaboration, whereby joint ventures could be undertaken and accomplished. Hence, our finite Universe would remain underdeveloped, primitive, and there would be no Heaven, without heavenly cooperation made possible by hellish pain and suffering. In other words, you can't have Heaven without Hell. There is one exception to this, which will be explored down below.

CHAPTER 5

Aug. 8, 2017

The fame that all of us mind particles (MPs)/ mind soul string particles (MSSPs) have (because an infinite number of MSSPs knows us, because we've been around literally forever) can be called Random Fame, RF, or Random Infinite Fame, RIF. Here on planet Earth-Hell, most of us believe ourselves <u>not</u> to be famous. We believe ourselves virtually nameless, faceless "nobodies". This feeling that we're nobodies is part of the punishment of hell.

The reason for our belief in our own anonymous famelessness is that the outer-circle purgatites, are bitterly jealous of the inner-circle hellites and wouldn't stand for our both a) being famous and b) <u>knowing</u> that we are already famous. We hellites might say "hellite celebrities have to live with our wordly celebrities and we rarely tear them down tooth and nail," The Purgatites would respond "if <u>we</u> purgatites have to live with jealousy, it serves you inner-circler hellites right to have to cope with jealousy without going berzerk. The purgatites don't want to tolerate our being luckier than they are because they don't want us to feel as lucky as they know we are.

What I'm saying is that purgatites and Heavenites are hotly jealous and furious in relation to us "lucky" center-stage hellites. Presently we'll explore the ramifications of their jealousy, which we hellites are forced to tolerate. So, in some ways hellites are luckier than both purgatites and heavenites, even if we're not allowed to know that we'll be as lucky as our Presidents and Monarchs, but we will. In the long run Everyone will be equally famous and otherwise fortunate.

CHAPTER 6

Aug. 9, 2017

Within very large Universes only a tiny percentage of the soul particle (= mind particle) population are allowed by God (president of the Universe) to reside within the innermost planet which is hell. The hellites have the advantage of being (secretly) center stage celebrities. If we knew how special we are, the planet would cease to be hell, and the peripheral purgatites and Heavenites would become so furiously jealous of us that they would refuse to count off time and space against hell. Consequently, Heaven would cease to be orderly as far as time and space, and there would be no cooperation or collaboration between and among heavenites. Heaven would become totally chaotic. Hence, Heaven would be too chaotic to exist as Heaven.

So, in order to have an organized, hence, heavenly Heaven, you must have a minimally chaotic hell where the hellites are having enough pleasure to not commit suicide, but not so much pleasure as to commit suicide, by dint of knowing they're the chosen celestial celebrities of the Universe. If we hellites knew for certain that we were the chosen center-stage celebrities for the Universe, we would say, "We're not going to tolerate this, who cares about their tiresome, asinine jealousy, who cares about them anyway? Let's commit suicide and abandon hell so we can move on to our glorious destiny and mingle among our Heavenites who constitute our worshipping flock, because they are envious of our center-stage celebrity position".

CHAPTER 7

Aug. 10, 2017

One of the ways in which the jealous Heavenites hate the destined-for-divine-glory hellites is by depriving the hellites of virtually all science, technology and knowledge. Hence, the Stone Age. Progress is actually the gradual mollification of the purgatites and heavenites. After taking away all technological blessings, the anger and fury of the purgatites and Heavenites gradually dies down. Moreover, the Pugatites and Hellites have suffered so much over the millenia that it's hard to stay mad at them.

On the contrary the Hellites have given Heavenites and Purgatites entertainment in the form of tragic humor, vicarious pain and suffering and they have constituted a central reference point of time and space, whereby to order our lives such that without this sadistic humor, heaven could not exist except as a frustrating no-way-to-tell-time and no way to measure space place. All the same science, technology and knowledge that was taken away shortly after the Big Bang has been almost fully restored. So "progress" (versus prehistoric "antiprogress"), is not really about our brilliant scientists. Instead it's about Heavenites and Purgatites becoming progressively less jealous and furious in relation to the center-stage divine glory-bound hellites.

CHAPTER 8

Aug. 9, 2017

Every particle (P) is a soul particle (SP) or, synonymously, a mind particle (MP) or string particle (SP) or a person particle (PP). You are an SP. And all the inanimate particles that make up the chair you're sitting on are string particles (SPs). An inanimate object does not become a conscious being until and unless one or more of its string particles become(s) a person-particle by having one or more of its component particles having its consciousizer switch fully turned on.

There are three ways in which a PP can be famous. (I) <u>Random</u> fame whereby your PP, being immortal, always having intermittently existed and intermittently always will exist. Random fame is fame by dint of being known by an infinite number of PPs by way of intermittent immortality via an infinite number of PPs knowing you through infinite intermittent time. When you're attached to your brain-body pair, you're pretty much forced to live whether you want to or not. But once you're out of your **BBP**, you can disappear and reappear whenever and wherever you want to.

(2) <u>Center-stage fame</u>, whereby God chooses you(r) PP to live one or more lifetimes on the center-stage hell planet (e.g., Earth) of your very, very large universe (3) <u>Circumstantially-chosen</u> or lucky <u>fame</u> whereby a PP becomes famous within their assigned

hell. All earthly famous PPs are actually no more special than any other PP. For example, George Washington is no more special than you and I; His circumstances were simply luckier in a relative way.

No one except God, is any more special or any more ordinary than anyone else, because everyone, except God is equal. God created you and me in the sense that he decided to put your PP in your brain-body pair (BBP) and my PP in my BBP. The only way a Universe can be devoid of hell is if it's very small, but this principle will be explained below. In a very small Universe, everyone is assured to get a turn to be President, so there is no hateful jealousy.

CHAPTER   9

Aug. 11, 2017

Before we get caught up in any other theories, let's explore the idea that your mind is an intermittently incarnated and conscious or unincarnated and conscious immortal particle that can choose to exist or not to exist, and can take on any size, shape, color, texture and taste and is NOT your brain (ref. 1). Most people tend to think their mind and brain are one and the same. Our goal here is to develop an intuitive idea that your brain is an almost unconscious or subconscious mass of zillions of PPs that can age and die by falling apart into their component individual PPs and only one out of zillions of string particles is actually you, that is, your mind.

If you have two or more fully conscious PPs in one brain, then you have conflict between the two (or more) conjoined identical twins who share a brain (which cannot currently be separated) and do seem to experience conflict and frustration, which suggests that each of two somethings smaller than a brain have a will of their own. This suggests there are two minds who share a single brain.

When we say someone is "selfish," we think of one mind that is obsessively concerned with its own wants and needs, at the expense of anyone else's wants and needs. Is a selfish someone a single entity or a selfish collection of somethings? If a person is selfish, how many things is S(he) concerned with? Answer: just one. So, the self is just one thing. We know this intuitively. Therefore, yourself couldn't be a collection of conscious PPs. Your self must be just one person-particle, PP. Our intuition tells us that our self is one selfish thing. So, if all matter consists in individual 10^{-35} meter long string particles (=PPs), then your mind must be a single PP = MP = SP = soul particle = person particle = mind particle.

CHAPTER 10

Aug. 11, 2017

Every particle (P) is a person-particle (PP) which is a soul particle (SP) or, synonymously, a mind particle (MP). You are a string particle (SP) who is incarnated in a BBP for a lifetime. There are three ways in which a PP can be famous: (1) Random fame, whereby you PP, being immortal, always having existed actually always having flickered in and out of existence, who may be known by an infinite number of other PPs. (2) Center-stage fame, whereby God chooses you(r) PP to live one or more lifetimes on the center-stage hell planet (e.g., Earth) of your very large Universe. (3) Circumstantially-chosen or lucky fame, whereby a PP becomes famous <u>within</u> their assigned hell. All earthly-famous PPs are actually no more special than any other PP. For example, George Washington is no more special than You and I. His circumstances were simply luckier in a relative way. No one is any more special or any more ordinary than anyone else. God created You and Me in the sense that he decided to put you inside of your BBP. Someday <u>You</u> may be President of a large finite Universe. And then <u>You</u> may put various PPs in some BBPs within some other center-stage hell. That would be when it will be your turn to be President of some other extremely large, hence hellish Universe.

CHAPTER   11

Aug. 12, 2017

Let's review a bit, before we proceed. The intuitive way in which we know that the self is a single very short string-shaped particle (which can change its size and shape to anything at any time except that its size and shape are limited when it is incarnated inside of a brain-body pair/incarnated) is because we know that when we are behaving selfishly we are allowing ourselves to only be concerned about one thing: the self. So, the self is just one thing. And since all matter is made up of string particles, if the self is just one thing, then it must be just one string particle. And since a string shape is much more adaptable and useful in terms of interconnecting other strings (particles) than a spherical particle would be, your usual person-particle (PP) is a single string-shaped particle with potentially enormous, even infinite, surface area.

Modern physics knows that energy and matter are interconvertible ($e=mc^2$). So, if all matter consists in tiny string-shaped particles, then all energy must consists in dissolved string matter particles. Matter is condensed energy and energy is dissolved matter. Therefore, your mind is a single string particle and your pleasure-energy is a dissolved, gaseous or liquified version of that.

CHAPTER 12

Aug. 13, 2017

Large universes are so large that they virtually have no outer boundaries. Hence, it is impossible to determine the true geometric center of a large universe. Consequently, God must arbitrarily choose one planet to be the virtual center of the Universe. This arbitrarily-chosen virtual center (but not actual center) of the universe must be fraught with suffering (the way our center-stage Earth is). And this becomes the center-stage hell of the Universe.

If there were no suffering in the center-stage, then planets like Earth would be Earth-Heaven, not Earth-Hell. And if it were Earth-Heaven, it would be just an ordinary planet and a heavenly Universe would have no reason to pay much attention to it or count off time and space against it. It would not command any particle attention, instead it would (unremarkably) be just another easy to ignore happy place. Earth would be just another boringly happy place that would go unnoticed and couldn't attract any significant attention. The existence of suffering makes the hell planet stand out so that the surrounding zillions of pleasure-drenched planets take notice of and get entertained by us, so it can serve as the geometric origin, 0-point and central reference point for all places and shared activities that occur in heaven. This is true in the same way that a movie that has nothing unhappy in it might tend to get ignored. Heaven is jealous of hell, because You, I and all the rest of us center-stage dwellers get a lot more individual attention than Heavenites do, and also because we Hellites have been <u>promised</u> a turn to be President of the Universe, unlike purgatites and Heavenites.

CHAPTER 13

Aug. 14, 2017

If we Earthlings knew how wonderful life in the heavenly periphery (except for relative lack of fame) is, we would be so envious that we would commit suicide or self-destruct in order to leave the center-stage hell in order to get to Heaven, which is peripheral to purgatory. Actually, Heavenites and Purgatites do have fame to look forward to, but it's set further away in time. Hence, we Hellites would be jealous of purgatites if we knew how much fun they were having in the periphery of the Universe and we'd be jealous of Heavenites if we knew how much fun Heavenites were having beyond the periphery of purgatory. And the Heavenites are almost intolerably jealous of our Hellite celebrity status, because their famous status is set too far away in time. So, hell is jealous of heaven and Heaven is jealous of hell. Suffering must exist in order to maintain the distinction between pleasureful heaven and suffering celebrity hell. Usually, there is only one hell-planet, surrounded by zillions of heaven planets.

CHAPTER 14

Aug. 14, 2017

This introductory first part of the book/essay might be helpful to some readers, but not to others. So, I'm going to start over, hoping that one or both introductions might be helpful to all or both groups of potential readers. Why did humans (MSSPs or person-particles, PPs) living hundreds or thousands of years ago nearby always believe in some kind(s) of afterlife and God(s)? Perhaps because their lives were so brutal that they couldn't believe that life here on Earth could be the be-all and end-all of existence. This life, tough as it was and feeling like a punishment for something (e.g., the love of fame, not money, because money is part of the punishment) had to be a precursor for something kinder and gentler. And overview of Earthly life tells us the goods and services we find here on Earth are so detailed and beautiful that some realm of existence beyond Our earthly ones would be necessary to explain how much pleasure and patience must empower the designer(s) to produce such intricate details. It's all too complex to be all by chance of the former. Evolution can only be a small part of intelligent design. Since fact is stranger than fiction, the latter must be a subsidiary, of some hidden agenda.

CHAPTER   15

Aug. 14, 2017

Your mind is Your Soul plus memories which is Your Experiences, which records whatever happens to You. Your Soul is Your records which can be effectively wiped clean of all experiences and memories, such as You have, such as You are, at birth. However, Your Soul's time machine keeps a record of all experiences and memories within its storage capacity, so Everyone can recognize everyone else based on their time machine's, storage facility. This way Everyone can know each other based on what past lives' content Everyone interacting with Everyone else can actually see and recognize within Each Other.

So, Your Mind = Your Soul plus Experiences and memories. But what is Your Soul? Your Soul is just one thing and it stays the same throughout Your life. Your Soul cannot be Your brain, because Your Soul is just one indivisible physical thing. Whereas Your brain is made up of zillions of individual subatomic particles. What if we tried to split your and my soul particle in two and then glue half of your soul particles to half of mine? Who would experience the lifetime of that hybrid soul particle? Would You and I both <u>half</u>-experience that lifetime? But what does it mean to <u>half</u>-experience something? It's nonsensical, because the two half-souls would repel each other and would search intently for their own respective other half soul particle.

I need to clarify that your time machine contents are not fully accessible to you or anyone else during your hellish lives, during which your <u>personality</u> is the only part of your past lives which is accessible to you and others. In purgatory and Heaven the full complement of your paste experiences and lives are what make you unique and readily accessible to you and everyone else.

I need to clarify that your Mind Particle = Your Soul plus memories and experiences. Your Mind Particle = Your Records plus your experiences and memories. Your mind = Your experiences plus your memories/experiences.

So, your experiencer = Soul Particle remains the same throughout your life, regardless of what experiences and memories do or do not get experienced by it. And even if you get Alzheimer's Disease, where your mind particle gets stripped of its memories, your mind particle reverts to being a single indivisible soul particle which is just one indivisible thing, which is still the essence of you, i.e, your experiencer, still the same identity, but will experience the life of an Alzheimer's patient.

Your soul experiences whatever happens to you and thereby becomes your mind particle. Whatever happens to you can be called your experienda and your indivisible soul particle can be called your experiencer, which is the essence of you. Next, let's experience why we think your soul, which is a physical rather than a metaphysical entity, is a single physical something.

CHAPTER 16

Aug. 15, 2017

String Theory physicists contend that everything and everyone in the Universe is made up of one or more relatively long (ten to the minus thirty-five meters) and thin (zero thickness, but that's impossible, because if a thing has <u>zero</u> thickness, then it doesn't exist as a separate object, so let's just say <u>very</u> thin) string-shaped or string particles.

If everything/everyone consists in one or more string particles, then your mind or soul, let's say mind-soul particle, MSP (soul particle plus experiences, memories and consciousness), being <u>just one thing</u>, must be <u>one</u> string particle (SP). So, your string particle = soul particle plus experiences = You, who is imprisoned within a big, cumbersome, inanimate brain and body, for a lifetime.

The difference between an <u>animate</u>, conscious someone and an <u>inanimate</u>, subconscious something is that the former contains at least one string particle that has its consciousizer switch fully turned on most of the time, whereas the latter does not contain even one string particle that has its consciousizer switch fully turned on. All of the string particles contained in an inanimate object have their consciousizer switches slightly turned on, so they can experience subconscious <u>pleasure</u>, the motivator of all life. For example, a computer is not an animate being unless it contains at least one string particle that has its consciousness switch <u>fully</u> turned on.

To recapitulate somewhat, a string particle, SP = a soul particle, = an experiencer. And an experiencer plus experiences = a mind soul particle = an MSP.

CHAPTER   17

Aug. 15, 2017

Some thoughts on why your MSP is probably not your brain are as follows. The fact that we refer to a single person as an "individual", "someone", or "anyone" embraces the notion that each person is one something unlike your brain which is composed of zillions of string particle, SPS.

Moreover, if we say someone is selfish, we thereby tacitly acknowledge that the self is just one thing, perhaps just one $SP = SP$ (string particle). We now know that despite being phenotypically very different from each other, a human being and a chimpanzee are genetically 98.5% very similar or identical. So, if genotypic differences don't account for the large ostensible difference between the two species, differences between the phenotype of a human being and that of a chimpanzee might be accounted for in terms of invisible differences between their two respective MSPs (mind-soul particles).

Also, if individual twins are actually quite different form each other, since the genes are identical, the differences between the two individuals may also be accounted for in terms of invisible differences between their two respective MSPs, since identical twins and clones have the same genes, if genes alone determined identity, twins and clones would be the same consciousness, but they are <u>not</u>; they are separate consciousnesses as much as any two organisms.

At least some cases of craniopagus, conjoined twins may be two consciousnesses or, synonymously two <u>m</u>ind-<u>s</u>oul-string-<u>p</u>erson-<u>p</u>articles (MSPs) sharing one brain. Hence, the two consciousnesses are not the one brain.

If the usual situation is one consciousness = one MSP bonded within one brain, the reason why upon dissection of the brain, we do see a large <u>polymorphic</u> object in the head (the brain), but no MSP, it might be that the MSP, (usually being no larger than a string particle, SP) might be too small to be seen. And the way in which the MSP interacts with the brain may be by means of the MSP traveling around inside the brain and body at very high speeds, possibly faster/higher than the speed of light as experiments in quantum teleportation suggest are possible.

Quantum teleportation can occur when two MSPs are positioned close together and the second particle observes the configuration of a faraway third particle. The first particle may consequently take on the characteristics of the third particle. And this happen hundreds of times faster than the speed of light. This phenomenon can be understood as a man and a beautiful woman positioned close together and the man and beautiful woman notice that the man notices an even more beautiful woman at a distance. So, in a spirit of jealousy and rivalry the first woman changes her configuration (looks) so that she closely resembles the faraway woman. Jealousy is so important because everyone wants to be the best and sooner or later will get a chance to be the best in the form of President of the Universe.

Maybe the thing that preserves your unitary identity throughout your ostensible lifetime is that a number, maybe 500, of string particles (SPS) stay the same and do not get replaced during the lifetime in question (e.g., Yours). But who would be experiencing the lifetime of the brain if we had 250 of your and 250 of my sps bonded in the same brain? Maybe You and I would both experience that lifetime in a drowsy, partial condition, even though the outward behavior of the hybrid organism might portray a very alert organism. This does not make sense.

If it does not make sense that a person could be walking around as one alert person who is actually two drowsy records working together, then it is an impossible situation. More probably You and I are each identified as a single mind-soul-string-particle (MSSP or more simply person-particle, PP) who is fully experiencing the life of a single brain.

Usually, when two PPs are bonded within essentially one BBP, there is quite a bit of conflict between the two who share one brain. So, a brain doesn't define a person; a PP does.

I believe Everyone should be acknowledged to have the right to self-determine when and painlessly how to leave our Earthly Life, but it should be noted that this route might be more painful than the natural route. By dint of being reincarnated onto Earth and/or additional time in purgatory and/or forfeiting a turn to be president of the finite Universe (God) which is determined by a one PP: one vote election that takes place at the end of the finite universe and initiation of a new such universe, following another Big Bang.

CHAPTER 18

Aug. 17, 2017

Aging is a process whereby an animate or inanimate object containing zillions of subatomic particles/string particles (sps) fall apart into their component parts, such as when a single person particle, PP's <u>particleplasmic glue</u> to the particles of a brain-body pair dries up and returns to the PP. But <u>You</u>, that is your singular mind-soul-string particle, MSSP or PP cannot age, hence cannot die, because You have no component parts to fall apart into.

But if your PP cannot age or die, then it has always and will always exist, on an intermittent basis. When it is pleasurized, it will pop into existence and when it is threatened with pain/suffering, unless it is bonded to a BBP, it will pop out of existence. When you're trapped within a brain-body pair, BBP, it is difficult to get away from the BBP, but when you're just a free PP in outer space or anywhere else, you can spring into consciousness any time the environment contains or is conducive to sufficient pleasure. You can drop out of existence any time the surrounding pleasure or pleasure-conducive circumstances are insufficient.

The reason why you've always been and always will be infinitely and equally famous is that if you've always (intermittently) existed, then you have made the acquaintance of an infinite number of intermittently immortal PPs. They've all always known you and you've always know them. In view of these considerations, if anyone asks will they see any particular loved one(s) after their all "dead", the answer is obviously yes. So, we're all already famous, even if the Devil and Purgatites are too jealous to let us know we're famous and center-stage to the Universe. And as long as you have the privilege of being center-stage and are in line to be President of the Universe, consequently, the Devil and Purgatites want our hellish lives on Earth to be miserable, so if they're going to take us seriously as markers of time and space, they won't have to feel threatened and insecure about us, as if we Earthling-Hellites were objectively more important than they are; which we're not.

To recapitulate somewhat, You're already infinitely famous, because You're infinitely old and know an infinite number of other "people" or MSSPs or PPs and they know you. So, you've known each other for an infinitely long time, even if you can't remember that because you're temporarily cut off from your personal, internal time machine(s).

The "laziness" of the poor, whether due to lack of interest or low self-confidence could be cured via learning/work-related and EEG (Electroencephalography), EMG (Electromyography) driven pleasurable brain stimulation as well as reproducible out-of-body experiences (OBEs) mental information sharing. These could cure the "lazy" problem by enabling everyone to (a) be interested in what they want or need to be interested in and (b) be powerfully self-confident in whatever ways they want or need to be self-confident.

CHAPTER 19

Aug. 18, 2017

I've always noticed that it took me much more time to do anything than it took anyone else. So, I've been convinced that I have learning disabilities and attention deficit disorder, even though my only two actual diagnoses have been obsessive-compulsive disorder (OCD) and bipolar manic-depressive disorder. In high school, I realized that if there were some way of injecting intense pleasure into any kind of endeavor, I could become fast and good at it.

Between my junior and senior years in college, during organic chemistry class I realized how to inject such pleasure into learning and working: Use a circuit designed in such a way that pleasurable brain stimulation would be delivered via implanted or noninvasive electrodes to one or more pleasure centers whenever your electroencephalogram (EEG) or other high level brain function indicators were to indicate that you were engaging in high-level mental activities like learning and/or working (ref. 2-12). But then I realized that electrodes implanted anywhere in the brain or central nervous system (CNS) might entail problems like strokes and hallucinations. So I devoted a lot of time to thinking about how those problems could be solved or bypassed. Pulses of ultrasound and/or electricity could be focused into any small region(s) or site(s) in the brain as though the obstacle of the skull and intervening brain tissue didn't exist by using time reversal mirrors and/or <u>TEMPORAL INTERERENCE</u>, whereby, for example, two or more beams of electricity focused from different angles through skull, if their frequencies were high enough so as not to interact with the brain, say 1,000 hertz and 1,001 hertz, there would be no stimulation along the two pathways, but there would be an effective stimulus of 1 hertz exciting the brain right where the two beams intersected in a small and deep pleasure center or other kind of functional location. So this might be how the skull and deep brain problems could be bypassed. Of course, there might be other ways, too. Temporal interference is not something I thought of, but because I don't have the full reference, I can't give full credit due.

CHAPTER 20

April 19, 2017

If, as string theorists contend there is only one kind of matter in the Universe (string particle substance) and if all matter is condensed energy/force, then there must be only one kind of energy/force in the Universe (string substance, gas or liquid). And if pleasure augmentation drive/or pain diminution drive is a definitely real kind of energy/force, then it must be <u>the one</u> and <u>only</u> kind of energy/force in the Universe. So, all attractive energy/force must be pleasure and all repellent/repulsive energy/force is pain diminution. And all pleasure/pain diminution drive must consist in liquefied or gaseous string substance. If there is only one kind of matter (string particle) then there must be only one kind of dissolved matter or energy; i.e. pleasure augmentation/pain diminution drive.

CHAPTER 21

Aug. 19, 2017

The Universe is infinitely large and contains an infinite number of finite Universes, of which ours is only one, whose center-stage planet is Earth-Hell. Each finite Universe is Big-Bang-Cyclical in nature by virtue of undergoing an infinite succession of big bangs. Let's focus our attention on just one finite Universe. Because it has no fixed outer boundaries, it must be defined at an arbitrary center point.

Each big bang starts with God choosing a point in the Universe and saying: "And the next center of the Universe will be this relatively small planet right here (e.g., Earth-Hell) as he points to the arbitrarily chosen center point planet and indicates where the next creative big bang will occur.

Since everyone wants to be the best (President) via the centerstage of the big bang explosion, when the big bang actually occurs, there is a tremendous bang as zillions of mind-soul-string-person-particles, MSSPPs or PPs knock their consciousness switches together at the divinely-chosen center point.

God allows two populations to enter the expanding center point. The center-centerstage gets populated by MSSPPs op PPs who are <u>promised</u> that they will get a turn to be President. The outer-peripheral, outer-spatial centerstage gets populated by PPs who are told they may or may <u>not</u> get a turn to be President, because of limitations of time and space within the finite Universe. The outer-circlers, led by the Devil (the Selfish Tyrant) threaten God that if the lives of the inner-circlers are not hellish enough, they will not cooperate with centerstage planet hell being time=0, x=0, y=0, and z=0, and consequently, there will be only chaos and no Heaven, Purgatory or Hell.

There is one case where there can be no suffering in a finite Universe, but we'll touch on that case later. Maybe it's late enough now in general, every finite Universe needs to have suffering within the central reference point planet. There must be a God-chosen central reference point planet, because the PPs couldn't cooperate in any ways unless they had a central-reference point planet and angry outer circle of PPs (MSSPs) who are so angry and bitterly jealous of the MSSPs who will definitely get a turn to be God, so that the furious outer-circlers take away all science, technology and knowledge, as a jealous punishment directed against the center-stage inner circlers, and leave them with nothing but caves to live in. This is the tragic beginning of the big bang cycle.

The good news is we'll all eventually be rich via pleasurable mind or brain stimulation that will be delivered <u>if and only if</u> and <u>when and only when</u> the mind or brain is emitting rhythms that are indicative of learning and work. Money will become obsolete because goods and services will be so much fun to produce that everyone will want to give them away. Between mind-brain stimulation and reproducible out-of-body experiences, everyone will be a genius by dint of everyone having access to everyone else's knowledge. So, we'll all know what everyone knows.

CHAPTER   22

Aug. 18, 2017

This way, the outer-circlers (purgatites who might or might not get a turn to be President) make sure that the inner-circlers (hellites) who will get a turn to be President have lives that are fraught with suffering and prehistoric cave-person misery. If you say how can our contemporary suffering compare with the cave days? It's true the early days were worse hell and the contemporary disappointments are better hell, reflecting that the outer-circlers (Purgatites) are a lot less angry now and they gradually experience restoration of more and more science, technology and knowledge, i.e., "progress".

If the inner-circle hellites weren't miserable, their planet would be just another happy planet that all of the outer circles (purgatites) would just ignore as a central reference point and no xzy cooperation would be possible. So, you need to have suffering, so the outer-circle purgatites will pay attention to and be entertained by inner-circle hellites' misery.

If the lives of the inner-circlers (hellites; e.g., Us) weren't more hellish than the lives of the outer-circlers (purgatites), then the latter would pay no attention to the former, and the inner-circlers could not serve as a central reference point of time and space, whereby the outer-circlers could cooperate and collaborate with each other.

Hence, without suffering, there would be nothing but spatial and chronological chaos. In general, the inner circlers need suffering in order not to have chaos. Moreover since chaos is generally pleasureless and painful, most particles wouldn't even bother to exist and you wouldn't even have chaos, you would just have huge expanses of empty space and time.

The only way you can do without suffering is if you have small finite Universes, where everyone can be assured of a turn to be President and the centerstage planet can be clearly marked as such and since it's not far away, it takes very little effort to pay attention to it. However, in general, the inner circlers need suffering in order not to have chaos or empty nothingness. We contemporary Earthling MSSPs are the inner-circlers in a finite Universe. The outer circlers (purgatites) and Heavenites are invisible to us in order to increase our suffering and to prevent our committing suicide out of envy of Heavenites and purgatites.

The outer-circlers (purgatites) are entertained and amused by our inner circler suffering. Hence, Earth is center stage Hell within the central reference point of purgatory. Earth and inner-circler space comprise hell, while outer-circlers and outer circle volumes of space encircling hell comprise purgatory.

One of the Hellish problems of writing anything is that our thoughts rush ahead much faster than our writing hand(s) can move.

CHAPTER 23

Aug. 20, 2017

We have already delineated the role of God in initiating a finite Universe, but a fuller explanation will be offered below. God creates all of the center stage creatures only in that He assigns each inner-circler and each yet-to-be-born purgatite outer-circler MSSP to the brain/body pair where S (he) will spend a lifetime. At this early stage in a finite Universe's life cycle, you have hell-bound inner-circler sufferers (like Us), outer-circler angrily jealousy purgatite sufferers like all of Us who have already lived and died or are yet to be born, yet to suffer a finite lifetime in hell, plus those MSSPs/PPs, who are outside of all the finite Universes in the interstitial volumes between finite Universes where there is Heaven for all and no suffering.

A computer, robot, chair or anything else could be conscious and animate if it contained at least one fully conscious MSSP/PP. Heaven is in the space between finite Universes.

CHAPTER 24

Aug. 21, 2017

All of us will spend a certain variable amount of time in hell/as hellites, purgatory/as purgatites and Heaven/as Heavenites. The least eager to be President or even center-stage celebrities (in hell), will spend the greatest amount of time being contentedly happy in Heaven. The most eager to be God and center-stage celebrities (in hell), will spend the greatest amount of time being tormented in hell and purgatory.

The amounts of each of the three kinds of fame (① famous throughout the infinite Universe, ② center-stage celebrity throughout finite Universe, ③ worldly celebrity like Hillary Clinton and Donald Trump, throughout or within the hell of a finite Universe) varies across space and time lines, $x=0^+\rightarrow\infty$ and $z=0^+\rightarrow\infty$, and $+=0^+$. Through infinity and immortality all of these parameters will be infinite for everyone, but not all infinities are equal; some are bigger than others, e.g., imagine you have a hotel with an infinite number of rooms and you rent out 10% of them to me. Your retained 90% of hotel rooms will be an infinite number nine times bigger than the 10% infinity that I have rented.

In hell, you'll be an inner-circler (within the central reference point hell), then a finite universe dweller in purgatory, then a Heaven dweller in the space outside of all finite Universes. Then the cycle will repeat itself, over and over again, forever, Heaven-Hell-Purgatory-Heaven..., at least until you learn to stay away from big bangs, hells and purgatories.

As soon as the inner-circlers are assured they'll each get a turn to be President of their finite Universe and as soon as the Purgatitic outer-circlers are assured they might or might not get a turn to be President of their finite Universe, they might all realize that from now on they should only go forward toward Small-Bang-Small-Finite-Universes where the size is so small that everyone can and will get a turn to be President of the Universe, hence, there will be no jealousy and, consequently, no suffering.

The outer-circlers (in large finite Universe) are so angrily jealous of the inner-circlers (who get to be such just by chance) that they threaten not to cooperate unless as a punishment to the inner-circlers all science, technology and knowledge are taken away from the inner-circlers so the latter will be forced to live a crude cave-dwelling, hellish existence. The punitive taking away of all science, etc. can be called <u>antiprogress</u> or <u>regress</u>.

What happens when you die as a hellite: You go to purgatory, but it's partially heavenized by the knowledge that you will be going to Heaven after you have your turn to be President of the Universe.

Over the decades, centuries and millennia, the outer-circler purgatites gradually cool off, get less jealous and allow God/President of the Universe to restore science, technology, etc. The restoration of knowledge and ability to the inner-circlers (in Our case, Earth Dwellers) can be called <u>progress</u>. Now speeding up from the birth of the finite Universe to the present early 21st century, we think we have a lot of science, etc., but the full amount of what was taken away will probably be restored between 2100 and 2150.

CHAPTER 25

Aug. 22, 2017

Following progress up through our current 2017+ era, we begin to realize that although personal money used to be proportional to effort, in our current 2017 era, it is <u>not</u> true that money is proportional to effort. What seems to be true is that money seems to make money, irrespective of effort. To be fair, in the work place, the people who effortfully experience the most stress (pain) should get the most money. But what if you could completely remove the element of effort from learning and working Effortless, ecstatically pleasurable learning and working would <u>not</u> be tedious learning and working, they would be play or recreation, instead. And being so productive of goods and services, people would tend to generate a lot of money for everyone. According to old ideas (consistent with them) that are no longer true, the most unpleasant, stressful and painful work should bring in the most money. And that's not really true in 2017.

In another 50 to 100 years, learning and working will become so effortless and pleasureful via brain stimulation, neuromodulation, temporal interference, time reversal mirrors, etc. that goods and services will be so plentiful that everyone can have virtually any and all material goods and services without money or effortful learning/working being involved in any way.

Hence, in 50 to 100 years, money and the dilemma between rich and poor (which one should you help more?) will be obsolete, because everyone will be effortlessly/ pleasurably rich/wealthy and there will be no poverty or even financial stress.

The problems of the Poor are often unfairly dismissed as laziness either of the low or lack of interest type or of the low self-confidence type. Pleasurable brain stimulation or neuromodulation driven by learning or working indicative brain waves could cure either type of deficiency. Reproducible out of body experiences (OBES), via enormous information sharing, could cure these deficiencies even more dramatically.

CHAPTER 26

Aug. 23, 2017

In 50 to 100 years, there will be tightly interconnected mind-soul-string-particles/MSSPs or person-particle/ PPs, so everyone (the World's population, including all past, present and future PPs) will participate in collective consciousness via brain stimulation, temporal interference, etc. Everyone will experience everyone else's wants and needs, via pseudo psychiatric interconnective extensions, as though they were their own. Therefore, everyone will love everyone else and will <u>almost</u> have full Heaven in purgatory (hell will be gone), all except for the painful thought that not everyone will get a turn to be God in the foreseeable future.

Reproducible (electro-magnetically and acoustically-produced) out-of-body experiences (OBEs) will be instrumental in effecting collective consciousness. And these OBEs will begin in 0 to 100 years. The election of a new president of the finite Universes (God) will be done when everyone will love everyone else and therefore be least biased in our voting.

CHAPTER 27

Aug. 23, 2017

A hellite is an inner circler PP. A purgatite is an <u>outer</u> circler PP. A Heavenite is outer-outer circler PP, hence is a PP who lives beyond the borders of any and all finite Universes, in a state of harmless euphoria and ecstasy. Next: why purgatory and Heaven are invisible to us Hellites. If you and I and other Earthlings could see how much careless contentment and fun Heavenites and even purgatites are having, we Earthlings would commit suicide in the fastest, least painful way possible, so that we could join our happy counterparts in Heaven or even purgatory.

So far, there is no proof such that an atheist would accept that Earth = Hell center of our finite Universe, but there's loads of suggestive evidence. For example, our pains hurt more than our pleasures feel good. Plus: anything on Earth can be more quickly and easily destroyed than it can be created.

Plus: many small objects of significant value, e.g., a diamond ring can be more easily lost than found. Plus: anything that can be much fun (e.g., drugs, alcohol, fatty, sugary foods, sex) can lead to painful problems and situations that are much worse than the pleasures that initiate them are wonderful. Moreover, here on Earth we are well-advised to "follow" and manage a balancing act between pleasure and pains. If someone gives you a compliment, that feels good. Most of life is stressful when we keep busy and boring when we don't. So, earthly life tends to be a balancing act between being stressed out but busy and bored but idle/relaxed. Sex is something we think of as a tantalizing good, but when you get down to the essence of it, most of it consists in foul odors, foul-lasting body secretions and unwanted pregnancies. Most of these bad things are things we accept and take for granted. We generally, don't give a second thought to them. But our taking them for granted, because that's all we're used to, doesn't invalidate them as stressors and punisments.

Plus for now, anyway, only a tiny percentage of us get to be really famous and extremely rich right here in hell, whereas around the end of the Big Bang Cycle, all of us hellites and purgatites will be <u>both</u> famous and rich as well as <u>blessed</u> in <u>many</u> other <u>ways</u> such as everyone loving everyone else, being a genius and having turns to be God within finite Universes.

CHAPTER 28

April 30, 2020

Your soul is a real physical particle which we may call a <u>mind</u> or <u>mind</u> <u>particle</u> (MP).

According to physicists who are superstring theorists, all matter is made up of one or more superstring particles, each of which is about 100 billion, billion times smaller than a proton.

If we suppose your mind or consciousness is your <u>brain</u>, then who would we be if you had <u>half</u> of your brain and half of my brain inside of the same skull and creature? I realize this is experimentally impossible at this time, but sooner or later, it might become possible. Would it be half you and half me? But the idea of <u>half</u>-experiencing something is nonsensical. So, you are not your brain. There are already conjoined twins who have two consciousnesses inside of one brain and this suggests that consciousness is smaller than one brain. But how much smaller?

In 1619, the renowned astronomer, Johannes Kepler wrote that the "soul has the structure of a point... and the figure of a circle..." couldn't he have been describing an enlarged and shape-modified string particle/mind particle? He wrote this in <u>Harmonices</u> <u>Mundi</u>.

Our intuition tells us our mind/consciousness is a single, indivisible entity. And if all matter (including your mind, which is both matter and energy, $e=mc^2$) consists in one or more superstring particles, then your mind (particle) must be a <u>single</u> superstring particle, which does not require bonding to a brain/body pair (**BBP**).

Not all superstring particles are conscious, only those with their consciousness switch turned on. If the switch is turned off, then the superstring particle is not a conscious-MP particle. Most superstring particles are not conscious.

Whenever we feel someone is behaving selfishly, we feel that the selfish someone is only concerned about <u>one</u> thing, such as one particle. Hence, the self is just one thing, such as one particle. It is certainly not billions of things, such as brain cells, molecules or even atoms.

If you could separate your superstring MP from your BBP, you would have an out-of-body experience, whereby your MP is conscious despite no BBP.

CHAPTER 29

May 1, 2020

God is the only physical entity in the universe who does not consist in one or more superstring particles. He fills the universe, except for an infinite number of <u>finite</u> universe-occupying spaces, because He doesn't want to be alone in the infinite universe.

God invented the superstring particle (which can be conscious), because He wanted conscious beings whom He could love and who would prevent Him from being lonely and bored.

Jesus is the son of God and He is a pseudopodium or outcropping of God, the infinite-space-occupying Father. Jesus, like His Father is capable of occupying an infinite amount of space. You and I are finite beings who can only occupy superstring particle space.

However, each one of us can be elected President of our respective finite universe for a finite term of office.

As President, we get elected by all of our sibling superstring particles. As such, we get a chance, now and then to feel super-special.

CHAPTER 30

May 4, 2020

I believe in a monotheistic God who is infinitely superior to all of the rest of us conscious beings, because I'm <u>afraid</u> <u>not</u> <u>to</u>. I'm afraid that if I unjustly belittle God, He will punish me, sooner or later, or both.

On the other hand, everyone wants to be the best and to feel super-special. So there is a dichotomy between a) a universe that seems fair and everyone there gets a turn to be God and b) a universe that seems les fair but better protected against suffering and insecurity, where there is a monotheistic God who always protects us all.

I choose to go with b). But if b is true, then why is there <u>any</u> suffering? The conventional answer is that suffering results from human abuse of free will. Then why do animals suffer and why do we suffer from epidemics and natural disasters, which don't seem to have anything to do with free will?

For example, why didn't God create a world where if you freely choose one thing, you get coconut cream pie and if you choose another thing, you get a butterscotch sundae? Why does there need to be a bucket of excrement associated with <u>any</u> choice?

CHAPTER 31

May 5, 2020

If God were all-powerful and all-good, then He would destroy the devil and eliminate all suffering, regardless of how we use or "abuse" our free will.

There could be a specific reason why God cannot get rid of all suffering and evil. This reason is explained above and involves earth-hell serving as a central refence point for pleasure-filled planets who are entertained by our suffering.

CLOSING COMMENTS

Fame and celebrity are slightly different because the latter unlike the former necessarily involves fanfare and being celebrated. In summary, there are three notable kinds of fame and two notable kinds of celebrity.

1. You're already infinitely famous because you've always existed (on and off) and you and everyone else have always known everyone else, so everyone is already infinitely famous because everyone knows everyone else, Celebrity is not particularly involved here.

2. Everyone is also famous throughout an infinite number of finite Universes, especially throughout each finite Universe's purgatory. There's more celebrity here because each hellite is known and celebrated by every purgatite.

3. About one in 1,000 hellites are also famous throughout hell (e.g., Hillary Clinton, Donald Trump, etc.) and, yes, this kind of fame involves a lot of celebrity because almost all non-famous hellites think that almost all famous hellites must be vastly more special than the rest of Us. It's angry purgatites who insist that only a tiny percentage of hellites can be famous within hell. The purgatites reason (?) that if they can tolerate our (hellites') being lined up for

presidency, then we hellites can tolerate the hurtful (and wrong-headed) privilege though the Clintons, Trumps, etc. are not really more special than we are.

Two kinds of being wealthy are:

1. Being wealthy in comparison to other hellites because of <u>brain stimulation</u>, etc tends to equalize everyone financially and make everyone wealthy.

2. All hellites, purgatites and Heavenites will be virtually infinitely wealthy because money will be obsolete via brain stimulation, etc. which will cure the "laziness" or lack of interest and low self-confidence, by dint of pleasurably obsolete, effortless learning, working and money.

Moreover, once you're out of hell, you may have or not have a body of your own choice to house your PP. That body could be as big or small as you like. You could look like Marilyn Monroe or Cary Grant or anyone else. Your body fluids could taste like and be candy. You could have male genitalia in front and female genitalia in back. Your body could produce no excrement and nor require or be equipped with a rectum, anus, etc to prove a point. Milk is a prime example of a body fluid that's already quite delicious.

Other applications of brain stimulation, temporal interference etc. would be foolproof, sleep and alarm clocks, effective appetite suppressors for obesity and time machines. Reproducible out of body experiences and time machines built right into our PPs could enhance our identities and enable others to recognize us by the contents of our time machines.

Everyone will be a genius by dint of unlimited learning, as a consequence of brain (or mind) rhythms that uniquely identify high-level mental processes that will be used as signals directed into the mind particle-PP which render learning ad working intensely pleasurable and render us hellites, purgatites and Heavenites extremely industrious and productive.

The original depiction of the Judao-Christian God was harsh and vengeful like early Cave-Man/Person hell. Subsequently, as life in hell became less hellish, God evolved into a kinder, gentler being. If we extrapolate the kinder, gentler idea, we find we have a God who thinks <u>everyone</u> including Her/Him <u>should be</u> in ecstasy all the time. Moreover, your soul particle or person particle (PP) is a real physical particle that conforms to the laws of math and science; it's not just a spiritual, immortal entity.

The way in which to make people more joyfully productive, hence wealthier, would be to use mind/brain stimulation in such ways that effortless, pleasurable stimulation would be delivered to the mind/brain if and only if and when and only when the mind's/brain's output rhythms indicate industrious activity. This would be essentially a positive biofeedback method. It would also be B.F. Skinner's operant conditioning.

REFERENCES

1. Swartz, Jeffrey M., MD. and Gladding, Rebecca, MD. You are not your Brain. Avery/Penguin. 2011, 362 pages.

2. Mancini L. S. How learning ability might be improved by brain stimulation. *Speculations in science and Technology, 1982;* 5 (1): 51-53.

3. Mancini L. S. Brain stimulation to treat mental illness and enhance human learning, creativity, performance, altruism and defenses against suffering. *Medical Hypothesis, 1986;* 21: 209-219.

4. Mancini L. S. Riley-Day Syndrome, brain stimulation and the genetic engineering of a world without pain. *Medical hypothesis* 1990; 31: 201-207.

5. Mancini L. S. Ultrasonic antidepressant therapy might be more effective than electroconvulsive therapy (ECT) in treating severe depression. Medical Hypothesis, 1992; 38: 350-351.

6. Mancini L. S. A magnetic choke-saver might relieve choking. *Medical Hypothesis,* 1992; 38: 349.

7. Mancini L. S. A proposed method of pleasure-inducing biofeedback using ultrasound stimulation of brain

structures to enhance selected EEG states. *Speculations in science and Technology*, 1993; <u>16</u> (1): 78-79.

8. Mancini L. S. (written under the pseudonym Nemo Tee Noon, MD). Waiting hopefully. *Western New York Mental Health World*, 1995; <u>3</u> (4), Winter: 14.

9. Mancini L. S. How Everyone could be Rich, Famous, Etc., Trafford Publishing, 2006; 240 pages.

10. Mancini L. S. How we'll all be Equally Rich Famous, Brilliant Etc., Forever, Trafford Publishing, 2010; 190 pages.

11. Kaku, Michio. Hyperspace: A Scientific Odyssey Through Parallel Universes. Time Warps, and the 10th Dimension. Anchor Books, Doubleday, Oxford University Pres, 1994, 360 pages: p. 87

God always did and always will exist. But if Everyone, including God, is equal, then You always did and always will exist, too. But if You always did exists, then an infinite number of souls have known You, therefore, You and Everyone else are infinitely famous. So fame is not a rare commodity except on Earth-hell. And You, God, and Everyone else is a cosmic celestial celebrity. There are three kinds of Fame: (1) Immortality-related, (2) Secret Celebrity while You live in center-stage hell, and (3) Celestial Celebrity after You leave hell (e.g., Earth) and are told You've been a celebrity all along. And there two kinds of effortless learning, working and money. The first is pleasurable mind/brain-stimulated learning, etc. And the second is reproducible out-of-body-experiential circulation, whereby all knowledge will belong to Everyone and Everyone will love Everyone else.

Lewis S. Mancini, M.D. is a psychiatrist with additional background in biophysics, bio engineering, and electroencephalography (EEG) technology. He was a psychiatrist-in-training in 1985 when a combination of obsessive-compulsive disorder, manic depression, and learning disabilities derailed his plans. He hopes to return to his original plans when and if effective treatments become available to him.

Printed in the United States
By Bookmasters